Discard

For Georgia, and the
everyday heroes who
fight for justice
—DR

For my mom,
an activist with
a sweet tooth
—LF

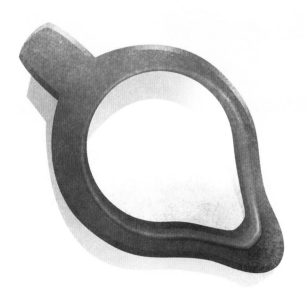

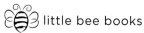 little bee books

An imprint of Bonnier Publishing USA
251 Park Avenue South, New York, NY 10010
Text copyright © 2018 by Deanna Romito
Illustrations copyright © 2018 by Laura Freeman
Pound cake recipe used with permission from NPR's Kitchen Sisters.
Library of Congress Cataloging in Publication Data is available upon request.
Manufactured in China   HUH 0818
First Edition   10 9 8 7 6 5 4 3 2 1
ISBN 978-1-4998-0720-2

littlebeebooks.com
bonnierpublishingusa.com

PIES FROM NOWHERE

HOW GEORGIA GILMORE SUSTAINED THE MONTGOMERY BUS BOYCOTT

BY DEE ROMITO

ILLUSTRATED BY LAURA FREEMAN

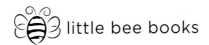 little bee books

When Georgia Gilmore was a young girl, she lived on a farm in Alabama where she fed the pigs and milked the cows. Georgia did her best to listen to what her mother taught her: Think twice before doing anything you might regret, and never, ever hate anyone.

Georgia grew up and soon had a family of her own. She did plenty of cooking along the way, and when it was time for something sweet, she knew just what to do.

She'd blend butter and sugar in a bowl to get her homemade pound cake started and then add tea bags to a pot of water for a new batch of sweet tea.

Georgia was a cook at the National Lunch Company in downtown Montgomery, Alabama. Because of segregation laws, the restaurant counter was separated into two sections.

One side for white customers.

APPLE PIE 10¢ GRILLED CHEESE 10¢ CHICKE SALA

One side for black customers.

Georgia knew it was wrong, but that was the way things had always been.

On December 1, 1955,
Georgia was working at
the restaurant when a news
alert came over the radio.
An African American woman
named Rosa Parks had been
arrested for refusing to
give up her seat on a bus
to a white passenger.

Rosa was tired of giving in to rules that were unjust.
And she wasn't the only one.

The next day, a flyer was passed around the Black community in Montgomery, asking people to boycott public transportation on Monday. It said, "Please stay off of all buses!"

Georgia watched as buses drove down the street, one after another.

Empty.

Empty.

Empty.

Because she'd been treated poorly by the drivers
so many times before, Georgia hadn't ridden the
buses for two months. Still, she wanted to
be a part of the movement she saw growing.

Not long after, she went to Holt Street Baptist Church to hear Dr. Martin Luther King Jr. speak.

The church was full. The crowd overflowed onto the street outside. Large speakers had been set up so everyone could hear.

Dr. King spoke about doing good things for one another.

He talked about freedom.

Unity.

Equality.

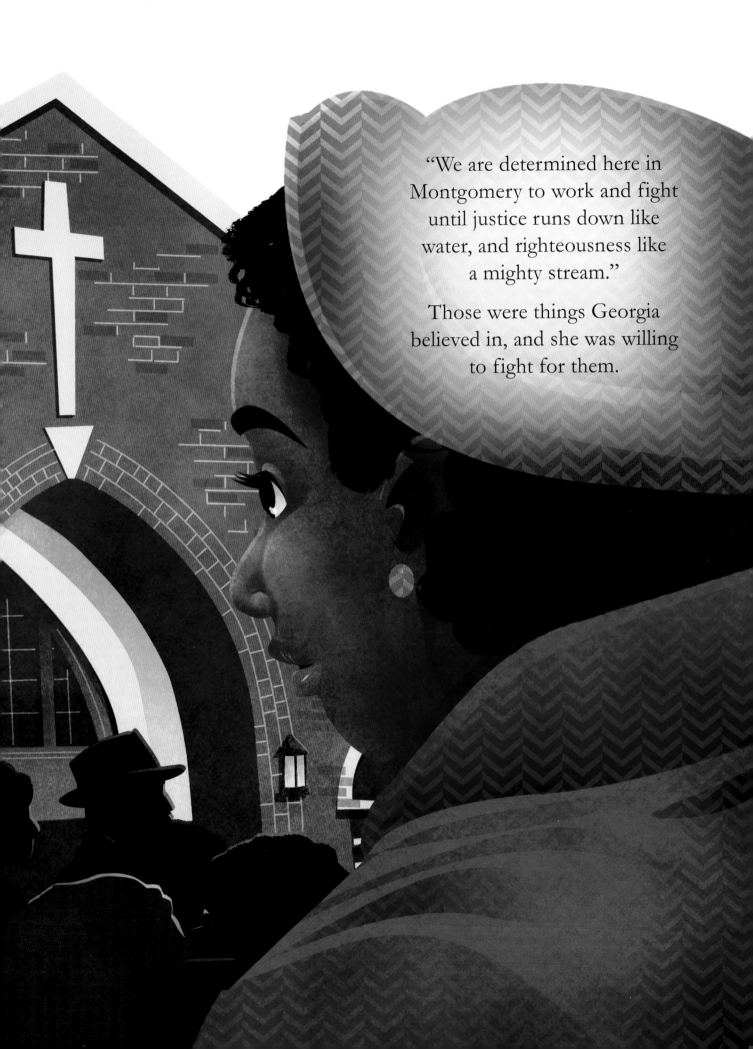

"We are determined here in Montgomery to work and fight until justice runs down like water, and righteousness like a mighty stream."

Those were things Georgia believed in, and she was willing to fight for them.

So Georgia decided to help the best way she knew how.

She worked with a group of women, and together, they purchased the supplies they needed—bread, lettuce, and chickens.

And then off they went to cook.

The women brought food to the meetings that followed at the church. They sold sandwiches.

They sold dinners in their neighborhoods.

As the bus boycotters walked and walked, Georgia cooked and cooked. And boy, did the people of Montgomery love her food!

Georgia's group donated the profits from their sales to the Montgomery Improvement Association, which helped fund the boycott.

But if anyone had found out these women were involved, they could have lost their jobs!

So Georgia ran the operation, and the other women acted as secret helpers.

"See, the way I figured it, people always had to eat. So I made the pies," said Georgia.

The women sold baked goods to local stores, groceries, laundromats, and beauty shops, and people paid in cash so they wouldn't be connected to aiding the boycott.

Sweet potato pie.

Peach pie.

Red velvet cake.

7-up cake.

Only Georgia knew who baked them, and only Georgia knew who bought them.

Every Monday and Thursday, Georgia would go early to the boycott strategy meetings at the church. She'd walk up to the collection plate and announce how much her group was contributing.

There was cheering.

Clapping.

Foot stomping!

But whenever people asked where the money came from, she remembered her promise to keep it a secret.

"It came from nowhere," she'd say.

Because of this, her brave group of women bakers became known as the Club from Nowhere.

The club not only raised enough to purchase gas for the carpool system that had been set up for the boycott, but they were also able to buy station wagons to aid the effort and help get people where they needed to go.

But Montgomery didn't want their buses continuing to lose money, so the city did what it could to stop the protesters and their efforts.

Dr. King and eighty-nine others were arrested for their roles in the boycott, and Georgia was called to speak in court about an instance when a bus driver had mistreated her. After she had already paid, the driver demanded she get off and enter through the back of the bus.

"When I reached the back door and was about to get on, he shut the back door and pulled off, and I didn't even ride the bus after paying my fare. So I decided right then and there I wasn't going to ride the buses anymore," Georgia testified.

Georgia knew she was doing the right thing by standing up for her fellow protesters, but news of the trial spread across the country like wildfire. When the National Lunch Company found out she was part of the boycott, she was fired from her job.

Georgia was unemployed and raising six children on her own.
She needed to find a new way to support her family.

Dr. King encouraged her to start her own business.
"All these years you've worked for somebody else.
Now it's time you worked for yourself," he said.

He helped her improve the kitchen in her home, and
Georgia got new pots and pans and cooking supplies.

Word soon got around, and people came to eat at Georgia's.

When they came to her house for a meal, they would eat wherever they could find a seat. And if they couldn't find a seat, they'd eat standing up!

Georgia loved to talk and joke with her customers and friends.
Soon enough, there were long lines to get a meal cooked by her.

People ordered meals for delivery too. Georgia was making hundreds of lunches each day!

She packed up fried chicken, black-eyed peas with okra, fresh corn muffins, and apple pie, and sent her kids out to deliver them.

If you were lucky, you might even get her homemade macaroni and cheese.

She was providing good food for her community, but she was also bringing the people of Montgomery together—black and white.

Dr. King frequently had meals at
Georgia's house. Because she was
a big woman with a big personality,
he lovingly called her "Tiny."

And because civil rights leaders
knew they could trust Georgia, her
home became a place for important,
and often secret, meetings.

"I just served 'em and let 'em talk,"
she'd say.

On November 13, 1956, Georgia was cooking in her kitchen, listening to music on the radio, when the station interrupted the song to deliver the news: The Supreme Court had declared that segregation on buses was illegal! The boycotters had won.

Georgia was thrilled!

People could ride the bus and sit *anywhere* they desired.

At the next church meeting, Georgia sat in her seat and listened as Dr. King announced that the Montgomery Bus Boycott was a success.

"We didn't have to walk no more," said Georgia. "Even before Martin Luther King Jr. got up there and told us it was over, we knew it was over and we knew we had won."

Still, there would be more battles to fight . . .
so Georgia Gilmore kept right on cooking.

Sources

Edge, John T. *The Potlikker Papers*. New York: Penguin, 2017.

———. "The Welcome Table." *Oxford American* 31. (January/February 2000.)

Gilmore, Georgia. Interview by Blackside Films and Media. February 17, 1986. "Awakenings: 1954–1956." *Eyes on the Prize: America's Civil Rights Years (1954–1965)*. Season 1. Episode 1. Directed by Henry Hampton. Aired January 21, 1987. Arlington, VA: PBS, 2010. DVD.

Hendrickson, Paul. "Montgomery; The Supporting Actors in the Historic Bus Boycott." *Washington Post*. July 24, 1989.

Jarrett, Vernon. "Raised Funds for Blacks: 'Club From Nowhere' Paid Way of Boycott." *Chicago Tribune*. December 4, 1975.

Nadasen, Premilla. *Household Workers Unite: The Untold Story of African American Women Who Built a Movement*. Boston: Beacon Press, 2015.

Nelson, Davia, and Nikki Silva. *Hidden Kitchens: Stories, Recipes, and More from NPR's* The Kitchen Sisters. Emmaus, PA: Rodale, 2005.

Robinson, Jo Ann. *Don't Ride the Bus*. December 2, 1955. Montgomery, Alabama. http://kingencyclopedia.stanford.edu/encyclopedia/documentsentry/ leaflet_dont_ride_the_bus_come_to_a_mass_meeting_on_5_december.

Tisdale, Rachel. *The Montgomery Bus Boycott*. New York: Rosen, 2014.

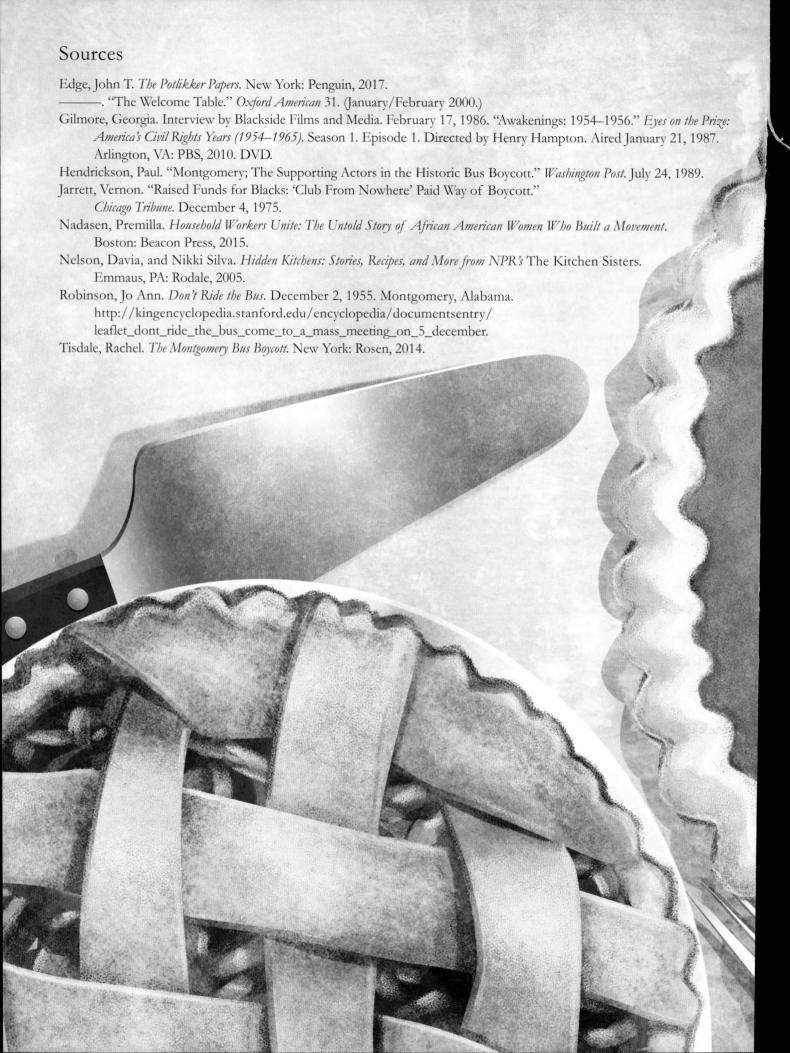

Author's Note

On December 1, 1955, Rosa Parks was arrested for refusing to give up her bus seat to a white person. At that time, Black passengers were only allowed to sit behind the COLORED sign on buses, and if more whites got on, Blacks had to move back. While two other women had previously been arrested for fighting segregation laws on buses (Claudette Colvin and Mary Louise Smith), Rosa's arrest finally sparked the Montgomery Bus Boycott, which began on December 5, 1955.

The city tried to stop the boycott by penalizing taxi drivers who charged less for riders who refused to take the bus, giving parking tickets to drivers aiding carpools, and arresting drivers and passengers for overloaded cars. Protesters faced verbal and physical abuse, as well as financial hardships. Despite all this, the Black community persisted. Many whites also aided the boycott by giving rides and making donations.

On November 13, 1956, the Supreme Court ruled that segregation on buses was unconstitutional. However, official orders weren't delivered to city officials for another five weeks. The boycott ended on December 20, 1956, three hundred and eighty-one days after it had begun.

The Club from Nowhere's fund-raising was an important part of keeping the boycott going, especially in the early stages. Their donations were critical in providing gas, cars, and auto maintenance to assist the boycott. They even inspired another group of women called the Friendly Club to sell food and raise money for the cause on the other side of town.

Georgia described herself as fiery and said that because of Dr. King, she learned to control her temper and made a lot of friends she wouldn't have made otherwise—both Black and white. Those who knew her described Georgia as a good listener and confidante.

Her home restaurant on Dericote Street in Montgomery became a safe meeting place for many civil rights figures. In later years, Dr. King even brought Robert Kennedy and President Lyndon Johnson to Georgia's. President John F. Kennedy once ordered her food for takeout to eat on Air Force One!

On the twenty-fifth anniversary of the march from Selma to Montgomery, Georgia cooked macaroni and cheese and fried chicken for those commemorating the occasion. But sadly, Georgia became ill and died soon after. After the funeral, her family served the food she had prepared—a fitting tribute to a remarkable woman. Georgia probably wouldn't have had it any other way.

"You cannot be afraid if you want to accomplish anything. You got to have the willing, the spirit, and above all, you got to have the get-up." —Georgia Gilmore